SNUGGLEBUG B⬤⬤KS ™

# Cownting

**Written by
Anne Miranda**

**Illustrated by
Barbara Leonard Gibson**

**TIME-LIFE FOR CHILDREN
ALEXANDRIA, VIRGINIA**

**1** cow baked
a chocolate cake.

**2** cows brought the spoons.

**3** cows stirred the lemonade.

**4** blew up balloons.

**6** cows hung the lights.

**7** tuned their violins.

8 cows dressed in tights.

**9 cows set the table.**

**10** arranged the chairs.

**20** little giggly calves
hid beneath the stairs.

# Great grandmoo was led to the barn, a kerchief 'round her eyes.

**Then everybody jumped at once and yelled a loud "SURPRISE!"**

Great grandmoo's birthday party
was really quite a sight.

**They ate and danced all afternoon . . .**

**and well into the night!**

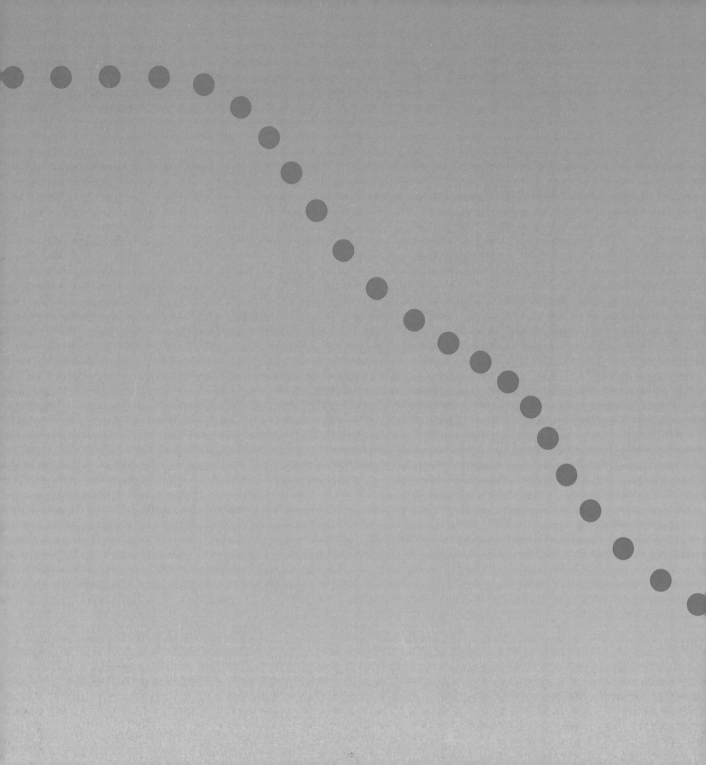